2004

A READING GUIDE

My Side of the Mountain

by Jean Craighead George

Hannah Mitchell

SCHOLASTIC
REFERENCE

0-439-53824-6

10 9 8 7 6 5 4 3 2 1   04 05 06 07 08

Composition by Brad Walrod/High Text Graphics, Inc.
Cover and interior design by Red Herring Design

Printed in the U.S.A.   23
First printing, June 2004

Contents

About Jean Craighead George   5

How *My Side of the Mountain* Came About   9

An Interview with Jean Craighead George   12

Chapter Charter: Questions to Guide Your Reading   17

Plot: What's Happening?   22

Setting/Time and Place: Where in the World Are We?   26

Themes/Layers of Meaning: Is That What It

  Really Means?   30

Characters: Who Are These People, Anyway?   38

Opinion: What Have Other People Thought About

  My Side of the Mountain?   44

Glossary   47

Jean Craighead George on Writing   50

You Be the Author!   52

Activities   54

Related Reading   57

Bibliography   60

"I can remember very clearly being
six and deciding that when I grew up
I would become an illustrator, a writer,
a dancer, a poet, and [a] mother."

—Jean Craighead George

Jean Craighead George considers herself very lucky to have had parents who supported her interests. They sent her to dancing school, made sure she had a writing desk, and even had summer and winter homes that satisfied their daughter's urge to ice-skate and swim. Early on, they encouraged her and let her decide who and what she wanted to be. Jean's mother and her aunt Polly had a motto: "Be different. Never follow the crowd."

In time, Jean realized that the greatest gift her parents gave her was a love of nature.

Born in Washington, D.C., on July 2, 1919, Jean Craighead grew up in a family of naturalists. Jean's family encouraged her to immerse herself in her natural surroundings. Jean found that she felt a close bond with the land and the animals. Her childhood was filled with experiences that inspired and influenced her writing. Jean's father was an entomologist, a scientist who studies insects. He often took Jean and her brothers into the wilderness along the Potomac River near their home. He taught his children how to make lean-tos and fish with homemade fishhooks and lines. As if she knew she might write a book about wilderness survival someday, Jean paid close attention as her father taught her where to find edible plants, as well as other wilderness survival skills. And the family all trained falcons, too. In fact, Jean's brothers were two of the first falconers in the United States. At the age of thirteen, Jean was given a falcon of her own to train!

At a young age, Jean discovered an outlet for her thoughts: writing. Jean has said, "I first became aware of the delights of the natural world when my father, an entomologist, presented me with what looked like a twig. When it got up and walked, my delight was such that I wrote a poem, 'To a Walking Stick.' I was in the third grade and have been writing ever since." In 1937, when Jean entered Pennsylvania State University, she discovered that her upbringing was different from that of her peers. "No one was more surprised than me when I got to college and found out that not everybody wrote and kept turkey vultures and owls in their backyard. I thought everyone lived with a closeness to nature. I wrote about [the natural world] because I knew it and loved it." In 1941, Jean graduated with degrees in English and science. Years later, in 1968, Jean Craighead George was honored by her university. She was named Woman of the Year.

Before becoming a full-time author, George tried several other exciting careers, including a job as a member of the White House press corps and one as a reporter for the *Washington Post* newspaper. She was also a nature writer for *Reader's Digest.*

No matter what she did, though, Jean Craighead George never lost sight of what she loved most: experiencing and writing about the natural world.

In 1944, Jean married John George. Four years later, she published her first book, *Vulpes the Red Fox*, which she cowrote with her husband. Jean kept writing while raising her three children, Craig, Luke, and Twig. When she was exploring nature on hikes and canoe trips Jean took her children with her. Jean took notes and made observations. Returning home, she would write while the children slept—turning her thoughts about the wilderness and the animals around her into the setting and the characters of her exceptional stories. Soon, Jean became well-known for weaving her extensive knowledge and love of nature into books for children.

Jean Craighead George has now written more than ninety books for young readers—among them *My Side of the Mountain*, a 1960 Newbery Honor Book, and *Julie of the Wolves*, which was awarded the John Newbery Medal in 1973. Although most of Jean's books are fiction, they have frequently appeared on lists of the best and most important books in the fields of social studies and science.

Over the years, Jean Craighead George and her family have kept 173 pets, not including dogs and cats, in her home in Chappaqua, New York. George has raised her own children to love the natural world. Each of them has translated their love of nature in his or her own way. Craig and Luke are environmental scientists, and Twig has become a children's-book writer, too.

Many of the events in Jean's books are based on her personal experiences. She continues to observe the wildlife around her home and incorporates it into her stories. "Most of these wild animals [near her home] depart in autumn when the sun changes their behavior and they feel the urge to migrate or go off alone. While they are with us, however, they become characters in my books, articles, and stories." Whether writing fiction, nonfiction, or picture books, Jean Craighead George has succeeded in bringing the natural world vividly to life for readers of all ages.

How *My Side of the Mountain* Came About

"Jean stared at the moss spores as though studying a painting...trying to memorize every detail so she could draw them later. Then she thought of other things the house needed: tiny acorn cups, for instance, and pine needle brooms."

—*Jean Craighead George* by Alice Cary

On a family outing in the Maryland woods when Jean was a young girl, she came up with an idea. As she wandered along behind her family, Jean found a tree stump with a little opening on one side that she thought looked like a door. Inside, the tree was hollow, and Jean began to envision a house. Only it seemed a bit cold to her, a bit empty. So she grabbed a bit of moss and laid it down inside to make it a little cozier. She was trying to make it a home. Many years later, when Jean wrote *My Side of the Mountain*, her main character created a home for himself in the same way, but on a much larger scale than Jean had attempted as a child.

Another important moment in Jean's childhood influenced her writing. In *My Side of the Mountain*, Sam says to Bando, "Any normal red-blooded American boy wants to live in a tree house and trap his own food. They just don't do it, that's all." For Jean Craighead George, the idea of a young person living independently was irresistible. She wanted to write about a kid who actually did it. In many ways, Jean's own childhood prepared her to write this book. One event in particular helped Jean create Sam Gribley's character. When she was a little girl, she told her mother that she wanted to run away from home. When her mother asked her why, Jean replied, "I'm tired of making my bed. I just mess it up again every night." Satisfied with that answer, Jean's mother encouraged her to go. In fact, she told Jean that she had better go pack a suitcase! And when Jean was finally all ready to go, her mother gave her a kiss good-bye and wished her a good trip.

So Jean left. She walked down the street and waited for a streetcar that she was sure would take her to her grandmother's house in Virginia. Jean never got the chance to ride the trolley from Canada, where Jean's family was living at that time. A neighbor returned Jean to her home and the open arms of her understanding mother. Jean was secretly glad to be back in her very own bed. Later, her mother told her that she had also wanted to run away as a child, and that her mother had even packed her suitcase for her! "I got to the gate of our yard," Jean's mother told her. "You got all the way to the trolley stop."

Throughout her life, and even into adulthood, Jean fantasized about running away and making a home for herself in the woods.

Instead of doing it herself, though, she invented a wonderful character named Sam Gribley. She has said, "I wrote eight books before I saw a way to get Sam out in the wilderness without the park rangers or his family coming to get him. He would tell his dad he was going to go to the family farm in the Catskill Mountains. Then I put myself in Sam's head and began to write using my own adventures, including eating all those delicious [wild] foods."

So *My Side of the Mountain* was born. The story, along with its sequels, has enthralled readers ever since.

"Great teachers and a few great
books make all the difference."

–Jean Craighead George

◆ *You have said that you were writing* My Side of the Mountain *for many years before you ever put pen to paper. When you finally did put it down, what surprised you about the story? Did it take any unexpected turns?*

The main problem was how to get him [Sam] into the woods in the twentieth century and not have people running after him. Then I remembered that when my daughter wanted to run away, I packed her bag and sent her down the driveway. Like Mother and me, she came back, of course. But, I thought, this is the way [to make Sam's story work]. So, Sam gets approval and off he goes.

Then another hurdle came. Although I had eaten all the foods Sam eats, trained a falcon, and all of that, I didn't quite know how to end the book. The ending surprised me. I didn't want him to go back to the city, and yet he discovers he's a social animal. And so I had the family come up. But I got an enraged audience. The kids hated that! They thought I should have left him up there! Mainly it was boys who objected.

♦ *Do you think it is possible to live like Sam does in the book?*

Yes, it is possible. Particularly if you have a falcon. A falcon is the perfect hunter. Plus, when we opened up America, we did that all the time—lived off the land. That's how we crossed the country. We didn't pack canned foods and frozen foods on ice!

♦ *Do you think that kids today still seek to conquer the wilderness? What about computers? Would Sam have liked computers? Do you?*

Well, there are always the kids who just love animals. Unfortunately, though, people have become afraid of the outdoors. Parents overprotect children now, when the best thing you can do for kids is to get them a toad or a guinea pig, or even a cat. Something to connect them to the natural world. So many parents don't have the background anymore to teach their kids about nature and how to conserve. So we are fast losing a connection. I think that's why *My Side of the Mountain* seems like a myth!

But Sam would love a computer. In fact, if he got his waterwheel going, maybe he could have one right on the mountain! No, he'd probably go down to the library to use it. I love computers. I think it is computers that are going to hold the world together.

♦ *You have said that, in 1959, your editor had trouble getting permission to publish* My Side of the Mountain. *The publisher was afraid of encouraging children to run away even with parental approval. Did you receive criticism for this? How do you respond to it?*

In a last-ditch effort to get the book published, the editor said, "Better that he runs to the country than the city, no?" And the publisher finally agreed! But no, I never got criticism. Not until very recently.

Now, I even get [criticism] from the kids. Some say no parent would let their kid do this. And I say, look, this is a novel! Every day I get e-mails from kids who want a tree—a world away from the adult world. The vast majority of kids, boys and girls, really like it.

◆ *How do you account for the actions of the adult characters in the book? Why don't they turn Sam in?*

There was an attitude at the time [the 1950s] that respected the child. We've lost this. I was respected as a child. If I wanted to go up on the roof and write poetry, that was okay. Maybe they [Jean's parents] thought it was silly, but they said all right, go ahead. Then, I learned it was too cold out there and I came inside!

So the adult characters in the book trust Sam. [The grown-up characters] realized he had an idea and they shouldn't turn him in. But they did keep an eye on him. They saw he was doing fine. Bando comes back—he never said he was there to check on [Sam]. But, of course, that's why he was there.

◆ *You have also said that you felt strongly about illustrating your own books, particularly the Sam Gribley books. Why?*

Because I lived it. You have to have been there to have it come across not only in the words, but in the drawings. I have seen a falcon fold her wings, dive, and kill dinner. That's why I am able to make kids feel like they've been there. I want to get them on scene. I can do that because I've really been there myself.

◆ *When you wrote* My Side of the Mountain, *did you know it would be the first of a series? Was it satisfying to continue the story—to write about what happened to Sam and his family as they started their new life?*

I had an aversion to series, so I had no intention of writing another. I thought one book was enough. But after about twenty years, my editor convinced me that kids wanted more, so I finally wrote the sequel, and then a third one. And the kids were satisfied. In fact, they still want more!

◆ *What is your writing process?*

I take notes when I camp or hike. Look up things in field guides. Talk to scientists. But I always write the stories at home. Otherwise, I'm too involved in the immediate. If I sit in the woods and start writing, it slows down the process. I come home to write, to keep the story going. I write the stories in my head while I wash dishes and do other chores.

◆ *You have said that you use nature guides to inform your writing. But what about fiction? What other kinds of books do you read? What did you read as a child?*

I read primarily fiction as a child. I loved Mark Twain, Charles Dickens, Edgar Allan Poe. My mother was a reader and read to us. But now, I really thoroughly enjoy reading nature guides and scientific journals. I find them fascinating. I see stories in them.

◆ *Did you always know you'd be a writer? What else did you consider as a career?*

We were always storytellers in my family. We used to sit around the table telling each other real-life stories. I loved to do this, but I never thought I would be a writer. That's why I became an artist, a dancer, a canoeist, and a swimmer. Then finally a writer.

◆ *What can you tell aspiring young writers about life as a writer?*

You have to like to be alone. Writing can be lonely, although you do populate your head with all these characters. You have to write every day. I kept diaries—every day. And you have to love it. In life, you just have to look for something you enjoy. It's hard to do a job well if you don't like it a lot.

◆ *What do you like most about writing for children?*

I like children because they just love nature. It's so much fun to have an audience that's so receptive and fresh. I still remember all my childhood books. I forget the novels I've read as an adult, but I remember those first books. They're very important.

I Hole Up in a Snowstorm

- When do you think Sam wrote the first part of the chapter? How can you tell this is a flashback?
- Why does he need to remind himself why he left home?
- Does Sam seem content at the end of the chapter?

I Get Started on This Venture

- Why is Sam so scared and hungry even after he catches the fish?
- What is the most important skill Sam learns in this chapter?
- What do you think Sam would have done if he hadn't found the man in the cabin?

I Find Gribley's Farm

- Why is it so important to Sam to find his great-grandfather's farm?
- Why do you think Sam's father wants him to tell someone in Delhi about Gribley Farm?
- Why is the meal Sam prepares at the end of this chapter so satisfying to him?

I Find Many Useful Plants

- When Sam decides to sit by the river and eat his mussels instead of heading back to his camp, what has he realized? Do you think this is a satisfying moment for Sam?
- Do you know what Sam's idea is when he looks at the big trees?

The Old, Old Tree

- What do you learn about Sam's personality from his early attempts to build a home and feed himself?
- Why do you think planning ahead excites Sam so much?

I Meet One of My Own Kind and Have a Terrible Time Getting Away

- Sam spends a lot of time making his tree house. Describe what you think the inside looks like.
- Why does Sam lie to the strawberry-picking woman? Do you think it was the right thing to do? Why or why not?
- Why is he so interested in the duck hawk?

The King's Provider

- Why does Sam set up a lean-to near the cliffs?
- Do you think it was mean of Sam to take Frightful from her mother?

What I Did About the First Man Who Was After Me

- When Sam sees the man by his tree, he realizes that he is not bound by anything, that he can leave the tree and find a new home if he has to. Do you think Sam would be sad if he had to find a new home?

- How does Sam begin to relate to Frightful?

I Learn to Season My Food

- Why does Sam think the weasel is brave?
- Sam tells the reader he was "too frightened to move" when the weasel burst out of the trap. How do you think you would have reacted in a similar situation?

How a Door Came to Me

- Why does Sam think it is okay to take the hunter's deer?
- Why does the "*pop, pip*" of the earthworms make Sam so happy?

Frightful Learns Her ABC's

- What is Sam trying to train Frightful to do? Do you think he will succeed?
- How does the deerskin suit help Sam live more comfortably?

I Find a Real Live Man

- How does Jessie Coon James help Sam?
- Why does Bando call Sam "Thoreau"?
- Sam is lonely when Bando leaves. How might you have handled the loneliness?

The Autumn Provides Food and Loneliness

- What makes Sam think about winter?
- Sam decides to stay instead of going home. How does he overcome his fear?

We All Learn About Halloween
- Why do you think Sam hosts a Halloween party?
- Sam tells the reader that "might is right." What do you think that means for the creatures in the woods?

I Find Out What to Do with Hunters
- Do you think it's okay that Sam uses the lost game for himself?

Trouble Begins
- Sam surprises himself in this chapter by doing what? Why is it unexpected?
- Were you surprised that Sam makes a new friend?

I Pile Up Wood and Go on with Winter
- Sam does not write about that first, awful snowstorm again. Why?
- Why do you think Sam is relieved when the storm arrives?

I Learn About Birds and People
- Why does Sam compare the birds in the woods to his neighbors on Third Avenue?
- Why do you think Sam is excited for Bando's visit?
- How does Mr. Gribley feel about his son's lifestyle? How can you tell?

I Have a Good Look at Winter and Find Spring in the Snow
- Do you think Sam really feels confident that his health problems will be solved, or do you think he might have actually been a little scared?

- Why does Sam cry when he sees the land peek through the snow?

The Spring in the Winter and the Beginning of My Story's End
- Why do you think Sam doesn't try too hard to throw Matt off course?

I Cooperate with the Ending
- Why does Sam open up to Matt?
- Is he happy that Matt and Bando want to make a guesthouse? Why?

The City Comes to Me
- Does Sam seem satisfied with the new arrangement at the end of the book?
- What do you think Sam will do next?

"Oh, this was a different night than the first dark frightful one....[N]ever have I enjoyed a meal as much as that one, and never have I felt so independent again."

—Sam, *My Side of the Mountain*

My Side of the Mountain is the fictional story of Sam Gribley's survival alone in the wilderness. The story is told from Sam's point of view and includes journal entries, notes, and drawings. Sam keeps an account of what happens to him when he leaves his home in New York City to live on his own in the Catskill Mountains in New York State.

We first meet Sam in the middle of a treacherous snowstorm. He is holed up in a tree he describes as his home. He has not been outdoors in days. Slowly, Sam reveals the circumstances that led him to his tree house.

Sam has had enough of the crowded, busy life he lives with his family of eleven people in the big city of New York. He wants a simpler, quieter life. Sam tells his parents that he plans to leave the city and live in the Catskill Mountains. He takes a penknife, flint and steel, a ball of cord, an ax, and forty dollars, and hops on a train. His father thinks he'll come back the very next day, so he lets Sam go. But Sam doesn't come back the next day.

When he gets off the train, Sam searches for Gribley Farm, his great-grandfather's farm that has been unoccupied for years.

In the beginning, the going is rough for Sam. In fact, Sam cannot even start a fire the first night. On his first full day in the mountains, Sam goes to the library and finds out where Gribley Farm is. When he finally locates the land where the farm once stood, he sets out to make a home for himself. Sam creates a place to live in the hollow of a giant old tree. He builds a bed out of hemlock boughs.

Having read many nature guides and other reference materials about living in the wilderness, Sam eats fish that he catches and berries and vegetables that he gathers from the land. One day, an old woman discovers him on the mountain. In an effort to make his presence there seem normal, Sam helps her pick strawberries. While they are out, he notices a peregrine falcon flying overhead. Sam decides to capture one and train it to hunt for his food.

Sam succeeds in catching one of the falcon's young. He names her Frightful and begins the training process. As he trains her, she becomes his faithful companion, in addition to being a wonderful hunter. Sam also makes other animal friends during his stay on the mountain, including a weasel he calls The Baron and a raccoon he names Jessie Coon James.

As winter approaches, Sam realizes he must plan ahead because food will be scarce in the coming months. He begins to stockpile acorn flour and wood. Sam also makes a deerskin suit from deer left by hunters in the woods.

Sam finds more than animals in his woods. One day, he comes upon a man taking a nap near his tree. Though Sam thinks that perhaps the man is a bandit hiding out in the woods, he learns that he is actually a college professor who took a wrong turn. Sam and Bando become friends and Bando promises to visit again at Christmas.

Bando follows through on this promise and returns on Christmas Eve. He says that Sam has been written up in all the newspapers. Bando shows Sam the headlines about a wild boy living in the Catskill Mountains. Sam worries that he will be discovered and forced to return to his home in New York City. Then, on Christmas Day, Sam hears his father calling to him. Sam is overjoyed that his father has come to visit. Mr. Gribley is proud of his son. He stays on after Bando leaves just to spend some time with Sam and to see how he lives now. When his father leaves, Sam prepares to live through the winter snows and cold.

At last, after a particularly dramatic ice storm, which Sam describes as having "sheets of ice binding the aspens to earth," spring finally begins to arrive. Sam is relieved that the worst is past and is excited for better weather, which will make it easier to find food.

Spring brings a host of new issues for Sam. One day he is surprised to meet a young boy named Matt Spell. Matt is in the woods looking for the "wild boy" who was written about in the newspapers. He wants to meet him and write a story about him. Though Sam tries to prove otherwise, Matt knows Sam is the boy in the newspaper articles. Sam agrees to help Matt with the story and lets him return during his spring vacation. At this point, Sam begins to wonder why he spoke to Matt at all. Sam thinks to himself that perhaps he wants human contact again.

When Bando comes back, he and Matt build a guesthouse. Sam realizes that he has started a city in the woods.

In the end, Sam's entire family shows up—all ten of them. He is torn. "I could cross to Asia in a canoe via the Bering Strait. I could raft to an island. I could go around the world on the fruits of the land. I started to run. I got as far as the gorge and turned back. I wanted to see Dad."

Excited to see his parents and siblings, Sam hugs his mother tight. They have not come to visit, but to stay permanently and make a home with him on the mountain.

Thinking about the plot
• Why does Sam leave home?
• What does he prove to himself on the mountain?
• What does he finally give into in the end?

"When the sky lightened, when the birds awoke, I knew I would never again see anything so splendid as the round red sun coming up over the earth."

—Sam, *My Side of the Mountain*

There are two major settings for this novel: New York City and the Catskill Mountains. Most of the story's action takes place in the Catskills. The author sets the story on a fictional plot of land called Gribley Farm.

It is 1959 when Sam Gribley leaves New York City to live in the Catskill Mountains, a mountain range about 100 miles northwest of New York City. The Catskills have campgrounds, summer homes, and resorts, but are mostly wilderness. The Catskills are called "America's First Wilderness." The region covers more than 6,000 square miles of mountains, forests, rivers, and farmland, complete with rolling hills, streams, and waterfalls, too.

In *My Side of the Mountain*, Jean Craighead George doesn't spend much time explaining what New York City is like, although she does say that Sam's apartment there was crowded. Eleven of

Sam's family members live in a single apartment on Third Avenue. And for Sam, that was ten too many.

George uses marvelous language to describe the mountain setting. She establishes the wilderness setting by describing it in great detail so that you can picture yourself there. "Two sentinel boulders, dripping wet, decorated with flowers, ferns, moss, weeds—everything that loved water—guarded a bathtub-sized spring." Plus, she includes drawings of flowers, birds, and other parts of the natural surroundings to help the reader visualize the scenes.

The Catskill Mountains provide a dramatic backdrop for a survival story. The varied terrain and the extreme weather make for lots of adventure and many challenges. When winter gets particularly bad for Sam, he writes: "Never had humanity seemed so far away as it did in those cold still months of January, February, and March." Delhi, the real town that is located near Sam's fictional camp, has some of the most extreme weather in the Catskill region, so Sam isn't exaggerating when he describes the intense winter and the exciting spring that follows. In fact, Delhi registers some of the coldest winter temperatures (an average of 14 degrees Fahrenheit) and some of the heaviest snowfalls in the Northeast. February is the most brutal month, with many days of temperatures below zero degrees. At the very beginning of the novel, we learn just how scary it might be to live through a powerful storm with such low temperatures. Looking back at his first winter days in the woods, Sam writes about his fear that he will not be able to escape: "I was scared and thought maybe I'd never get out of my tree. I had been scared for two days—ever since the first blizzard hit the Catskill Mountains. When I came up into the sunlight, which I did by simply poking my head into the soft snow and standing up, I laughed at my dark fears."

Even when March does arrive, temperatures regularly remain below zero. It isn't until April that Sam finally feels that winter is ending. The thaw begins and streams start to flow again.

Perhaps the most striking setting of the book is the tree in which Sam lives. It is the ultimate tree house, and the author details exactly how Sam goes about creating it. When he finishes making his bed, he describes it right down to how it feels. "The ash slats work very well, and are quite springy and comfortable. The bed just fits in the right-hand side of the tree. I have hemlock boughs on it now, but hope to have deer hide soon." The author even includes a drawing of the bed in Sam's journal entry. The combination of words and pictures allows the reader to experience Sam's home right along with him.

Despite Sam's talent for surviving in the wilderness, the author makes sure to remind us that Sam is a New Yorker. Mr. Jacket, who Sam meets at the store in Delhi, recognizes that Sam is from New York by his accent. Plus, Sam compares the birds that are his neighbors now to the ones he had in the city. This helps us compare the way Sam is living now with the way he lived before. It helps us to see the similarities, even though we might not think that there are any.

Although the book was written in 1959, Sam's story doesn't seem like it took place long ago. It just as easily could have been written today. Although modern parents are less likely to allow their children to go on unsupervised adventures, much of the story still rings true: The Catskills are still there—though perhaps a bit more populated—and the city is still as crowded as ever.

Thinking about the setting

- Where does *My Side of the Mountain* take place?
- When does it take place?
- How do the author's love and knowledge of nature show in the setting?

"He ate and ate and ate, and when
he was done he said, 'May I call you
Thoreau?'"

—Sam, *My Side of the Mountain*

The theme of a literary work is an important statement
the author wishes to make about life. In *My Side of the
Mountain*, Jean Craighead George explores several themes:
establishing a personal connection with the natural world,
asserting one's independence, surviving in difficult
circumstances, young people's search for adventure, and the
balance between the need for solitude and the desire to find
one's place in society.

Connection with nature

The most important theme of the book, connecting emotionally
to the land, is evident on nearly every page. In order to connect
with the land, you need to respect it and all it has to offer. And
Sam knows that in order to live solely off the land, he must trust
and respect his new surroundings. Without all the hubbub of the
city to distract Sam, he can spend long hours watching how the
woodland creatures interact with one another and with the

environment. From these observations, Sam learns how he can take advantage of the natural bounty to feed, clothe, and house himself.

As Sam establishes an emotional connection with the animals and plant life, he notices all kinds of wondrous events. Some of them are scary, some others are inspiring. These moments give him increasing respect for nature and its offerings.

Sam's observation of his first sunrise on the mountain sets the stage for the theme dealing with his connection to nature. "When the sky lightened, when the birds awoke, I knew I would never again see anything so splendid as the round red sun coming up over the earth."

After he captures Frightful, Sam's connection to his natural surroundings deepens. "It is hard to explain my feelings at that moment. It seemed marvelous to see life pump through that strange little body of feathers, wordless noises, milk eyes—much as life pumped through me," he tells the reader. From this we can see the affectionate bond begin to grow between Sam and his falcon.

Sam's observations reveal the depth of his connection to his new environment. In one instance, he actually takes a moment to admire the contribution of the earthworms, something he probably never would have done in New York. He writes his thoughts in his notebook: "I don't know why, but this seemed like one of the nicest things I had learned in the woods—that earthworms, lowly, confined to the darkness of the earth, could make just a little stir in the world."

When the winter begins to thaw and the mountain starts to breathe easier, Sam's connection is firmly intact. He writes, "Spring is terribly exciting when you're living right in it."

Survival

Not only does Sam connect with nature in many ways throughout the book, but he also must try to conquer it. As he observes the wildlife, plants, and changing seasons around him, Sam learns how to survive by making use of his knowledge. If he couldn't turn his observations into practical skills or items, Sam wouldn't have survived the harsh conditions. He must eat, keep warm, and keep safe. To do all of those things, he must conquer nature.

At no point is this better illustrated than when Sam finally makes fire on his own. "I must say this now about that first fire. It was magic. Out of dead tinder and grass and sticks came a live warm light. . . . Oh, this was a different night than the first dark frightful one. . . . [N]ever have I enjoyed a meal as much as that one, and never have I felt so independent again." He is overjoyed. With fire, he can cook and keep warm. Being able to create fire gives him the confidence to master other survival skills he will need in order to make it on his own.

Sam knows he needs a warm, safe place to live if he is going to survive in the wilderness. He gets a marvelous idea when he spies a giant old tree. A home inside the tree would keep him safe from all kinds of weather. It would also keep him hidden from passersby. Right away, he gets to work. "I scraped at it with my hands . . . I dug on and on, using my ax from time to time as my excitement grew."

During the winter, Sam faces his worst fears. In fact, the very first time we meet Sam he is scared that he will not make it through that first storm. Later we learn that he had provided for himself well. He had stored food, built a stove to warm his home, and even created a ventilation system for himself and Frightful. So, when the spring thaw finally begins, Sam knows that he has survived his ultimate test. This is a powerful moment for Sam. He tells the reader: "I looked down the valley, and in the dim light could see the open earth on the land below. The deer could forage again. Spring was coming to the land! My heart beat faster. I think I was trembling. The valley also blurred. The only thing that can do that is tears, so I guess I was crying."

It is Sam's ability to think ahead and think fast, his commitment to his goals, and his knowledge of the land that allows him to survive on his own. By the end of his solitary time in the woods, Sam has done more than survive—he has lived well.

Independence

The thing that Sam craves most is independence from his parents and his cramped quarters. He wants to be alone and self-sufficient. By the end of the story, Sam has achieved these goals. The first real test of Sam's independence occurs on the day that he is terribly hungry and has finally gathered a whole sweater full of mussels. At first, he heads back to his camp, where he plans to cook them. He suddenly realizes that there is no reason to head back right away and there is no reason to wait to eat. "But I don't have to carry them anywhere, I said to myself. I have fire in my pocket, I don't need a table. I can sit right here by the stream and eat. And so I did," Sam informs the reader.

Things that were easy in New York become giant undertakings in Sam's new life. It is the small things that test Sam's determination to be independent. When he wants to burn out the inside of his tree to make his home, he realizes that he needs a bucket of water in case things "got out of hand." He is in a predicament. "Where was I going to get a bucket? How did I think, even if I found water, I could get it back to the tree? That's how citified I was in those days. I had never lived without a bucket before . . . and so when a water problem came up, I just thought I could run to the kitchen and get a bucket." Sam finally understands what total independence is all about; he cannot depend on modern conveniences at all.

Later, when he comes upon the fire warden inspecting his tree, Sam again realizes he doesn't have to follow the rules he grew up with. In fact, he doesn't even need to have a permanent home, although it is convenient. "Then I realized that I didn't have to go back to meet the man at all. I was perfectly free and capable of settling down anywhere. My tree was just a pleasant habit," Sam tells the reader. Sam realizes that he can make a new home anywhere. He knows he can start again if he has to.

In the end, when Sam has the opportunity to run away from his family as they move into his new world, he chooses to stay. He has accomplished ultimate independence because he has proven that he can survive in the wilderness on his own. If he had to, he knows he could run off and do it all again. Instead, he chooses to continue to live off the land, with his family right there beside him.

Adventure

Many people dream of running away in search of adventure, but few actually do it. In *My Side of the Mountain*, the reader gets to live an extraordinary adventure along with the fictional character of Sam. Heading into the woods alone is quite ambitious and Sam's journey is chock-full of exhilarating moments. These moments keep Sam going. Learning to make fire, catching and training Frightful, and using deer for meat and clothing are important accomplishments. They remind Sam that he is succeeding in his great outdoor survival test and that he's having fun, too!

One of Sam's most thrilling moments comes when he must act quickly to get the prize a hunter leaves behind. "Without waiting to consider what I might be running toward, I burst to the edge of the meadow. . . . With all my strength I dragged the heavy animal into the woods. I then hurried to my tree, gathered up the hemlock boughs on my bed, rushed back and threw them over the carcass. I stuck a few ferns in them . . . and ran back to camp, breathless."

There is an adventure or challenge on every page of this book and Sam must find a way through each one by using what he already knows, paying close attention to his surroundings at all times, and learning from every mishap and every triumph.

Solitude versus society

At first, Sam is utterly content to be alone in the wilderness. He makes friends with the animals, talks to them, and treats them as friends. He avoids contact with humans at all costs, partly because he is afraid a stranger will turn him in, but mostly because he is tired of interacting with people. He learns to entertain himself, and is almost too busy to be lonely. Even in the winter, when Sam might have become overwhelmed by loneliness, he finds solace instead. "I did not become lonely. Many times during the summer I had thought of the 'long winter months ahead' with some fear. . . . The winter was as exciting as the summer—maybe more so."

Sam does feel lonely when Bando departs after his first visit. "I was so lonely that I kept sewing on my moccasins to keep myself busy." But then, Frightful strikes up a conversation with Sam. This comforts him and reminds Sam of the special friendships he has with Frightful, Jessie Coon James, and The Baron.

When spring comes and people start dropping in for visits, Sam realizes he has a need for human friendships as well as for solitude. "I worked with them, wondering what was happening to me. Why didn't I cry 'No'? What made me happily build a city in the forest—because that is what we were doing."

Thinking about the themes

• What is the main theme of *My Side of the Mountain*?

• What lessons does Sam learn from living on the mountain?

• Do any of the themes apply to your life? How?

Characters: Who Are These People, Anyway?

My *Side of the Mountain* has only a handful of human characters. The other characters are the wildlife on the mountain. Here is a list of characters, human and animal, followed by a brief description of each of the most significant ones.

Sam Gribley	twelve-year-old boy, main character, and narrator
Frightful	falcon
Bando	college professor and adventurer
Mr. Gribley	Sam's father
Mrs. Gribley	Sam's mother
Miss Turner	librarian in the town of Delhi
Jessie Coon James	raccoon
The Baron	weasel
The Barometer	the nuthatch Sam uses to gauge the weather
Mr. Jacket/Tom Sidler	boy from town
Matt Spell	teenage reporter
Aaron	vacationer/songwriter
Mrs. Thomas Fielder	the woman who goes strawberry picking with Sam

Sam Gribley: Sam is the main character in *My Side of the Mountain.* He is a twelve-year-old boy who seeks a different kind of life than the one he and his family live in New York City. He loves nature and wants to live in the wilderness, away from other people and material possessions. He leaves his family, intending to make a home among the trees, the birds, and the animals that populate the mountain. It is clear that he is a good researcher; he has a tremendous knowledge of the land. To survive, he refers again and again to information he has read in books. In addition to knowing which plants and vegetables are edible and which ones can be put to other uses, Sam has a natural ability to understand wildlife.

Sam's independent spirit thrives on adventure. He trains a falcon, makes a home inside a tree trunk, and cooks delicious meals of fish, animal meat, and wild plants.

Sam's connection to the animals around him grows as he gets to know their individual personalities. This is especially evident in his first encounter with The Baron. "I shall never forget the fear and wonder that I felt at the bravery of that weasel. He stood his ground and berated me. I could see by the flashing of his eyes and the curl of his lip that he was furious at me for trapping him. He couldn't talk, but I knew what he meant." In this encounter, Sam describes The Baron with the same words we would normally use for humans. Sam's keen grasp of animal behavior helps him understand what his animal friends want, even though they can't speak with words.

Courageous and confident, Sam almost always knows he will be successful. Even when he doubts himself, or becomes frightened, he never panics. He sets about solving problems efficiently and with ingenuity. When he needs to tan the hide of a deer, he finds inspiration in an old tree stump: "It had showered the day before, and as Frightful and I passed an old stump, I noticed it had collected the rain. 'A stump, an oak stump, would be perfect.'... So I felled an oak ... burned a hole in it, carried water to it, and put my deerskin in it."

The thoughtful way in which Sam looks around as he wanders through the woods gives him a thorough knowledge of his surroundings. Sam's cleverness at using the natural materials he finds helps him live better and more comfortably.

Over the course of the novel, though, Sam changes. At the beginning, he desires complete solitude. Slowly, Sam allows some people back into his life. Where once he would hide from anyone who happened by his tree house, later he becomes much more interested in interaction with other people. He seems to long for human companionship. When he realizes this, Sam begins to combine his old life into his new one. He questions himself constantly. Why does he go into town? Does he want to talk to a human being? Why doesn't he run from Matt Spell? Does he want to be found? Has he had enough of the wilderness? Sam has accomplished a great deal. Having ventured out on his own and established a very special relationship with nature, he begins to share his new world with the people he cares about.

In the end, Sam finds peace in his decision not to run from all the attention his new life has attracted. He is happy to teach his siblings how to live off the land. Though Sam is torn about his father's plan to erect a real house in the woods, and he is concerned about sharing his space once again, he is also content to be surrounded by a family that cares enough to change the way they live just for him.

Frightful: Frightful is a peregrine falcon that plays an important role in the story. Sam thinks of her as a good friend and confidante. From the start, Sam acknowledges that Frightful is a huntress with an independent spirit, so he trains her carefully. He does not allow her to eat her own kills. If she did, Frightful might realize she doesn't need Sam and he would lose her to the wild.

Frightful is a fast learner. The bond that develops between the falcon and her owner is one of the most touching outcomes of this novel. When he first begins to sense the falcon responding to him, Sam writes: "I looked into her steely eyes that morning and thought I saw a gentle recognition. She puffed up her feathers as she sat on my hand. I call this a 'feather word.' It means she is content." Later, Frightful communicates with Sam when she senses potential food nearby and when she senses danger. Frightful is expressive and loyal. It is her skill as a hunter that keeps Sam well fed, but it is her companionship that keeps Sam from feeling too lonely or frightened.

Bando: After a case of mistaken identity, Sam learns that his first human visitor is a professor who has gotten lost on the mountain, not a bandit on the run from the police. Bando is a relaxed, adventurous man who likes Sam immediately. Bando calls Sam "Thoreau," which is a reference to the nineteenth-century writer. The real Thoreau left his town life to make a solitary home for himself on Walden Pond in Massachusetts and live entirely off the land—just like Sam!

Bando admires Sam for creating a wonderful home in nature. He cares very much about Sam and is proud of his accomplishments. Bando does not return Sam to his family in New York. On his visits, Bando subtly makes sure that Sam is eating well, taking good care of himself, and is content. He becomes a good friend to Sam.

Mr. Gribley: Sam's father works hard to support a family of eleven, and from what Sam tells the reader, we know that his father takes time to talk to his children and encourage their interests. It is he who allows Sam to leave home to live on Gribley Farm. Of course, he does this thinking Sam will return the very next day. However, when Sam doesn't return, his father doesn't come after him right away. He has faith that Sam will be all right and is confident in his son's abilities and in his determination to survive.

At Christmas, when Mr. Gribley visits Sam, he has come out of both concern and curiosity. He knows that Sam is living as he said he would, because he has read the newspaper reports of the "wild boy" on the mountain. Once he sees what Sam has created, he is bursting with pride. Braving the hazardous winter also reveals the older man's adventurous spirit. Mr. Gribley extends his visit with Sam, partly because he has missed his son, but also because he wants a taste of the world Sam lives in now. He is so impressed with his son that he does not want Sam to have to return to the life he had before. He knows that this life is the one that makes Sam happy. When Mr. Gribley is about to leave after his Christmas visit, he tells Sam: "I've decided to leave by another route. Somebody might backtrack me and find you. And that would be too bad. . . .You've done very well, Sam." He takes a different route off the mountain in order to protect Sam from reporters who might expose him and return him to his old life. Mr. Gribley's actions show the enormous amount of respect and faith he has in his son.

In the end, Mr. Gribley leads the entire Gribley family to Sam's mountain home. This move shows that Sam's parents and siblings are both loyal and adventurous—traits Sam shares and displays throughout the book.

Thinking about the characters

- In your own words, how would you describe Sam Gribley? Can you relate to him? Would you be friends with someone like him? Why or why not?
- How does the author show that Frightful is Sam's friend?
- How does the author let us know that the adult characters are concerned about Sam's safety and well-being?
- In what ways do we learn that Sam is not completely independent, that he needs and wants people around him?

Opinion: What Have Other People Thought About *My Side of the Mountain*?

My *Side of the Mountain* is a hit with both kids and adults. Initially, the publisher had worried that readers would be alarmed that Sam's parents let him go off alone into the woods, but this received very little criticism. A few book reviewers said that the story was far-fetched, but everyone acknowledged that the story's themes and characters were marvelous. Jean Craighead George has said that her only criticism from readers was that they were disappointed that Sam's family joins him in the end!

Book reviewers, parents, teachers, and students agree that *My Side of the Mountain* encourages kids to think independently, to apply their knowledge, to pay attention to their environment, and to get comfortable with nature. As it was written in the *New York Times Book Review*, Jean Craighead George "provokes readers to a reassessment of their place in the natural world."

Besides receiving excellent book reviews, *My Side of the Mountain* has also won many awards. The most prestigious honor it has received was its selection as a Newbery Honor Book in 1960. The John Newbery Medal, introduced in 1921, was the first children's book award in the world. Its goal is "to encourage original creative work in the field of books for children ... [t]o give those librarians, who make it their life work to serve children's reading interests, an opportunity to encourage good writing in this field."

Each year, the librarians on the committee award one Newbery Medal. In addition, they also recognize other books that are worthy of attention. These books are called "honor books." The Newbery Medal and the Newbery Honors are the best known and most discussed children's-book awards in this country.

In addition to her Newbery Honor, Jean Craighead George has received other awards for her books. In 1991, she was the first winner of the School Library Media Section of the New York Library Association's Knickerbocker Award for Juvenile Literature. This award was presented to her for the "consistent superior quality" of her literary works.

In 1969, *My Side of the Mountain* won a George G. Stone Center for Children's Books Merit Award. This is given annually by a committee of teachers, librarians, and children's literature specialists for books "that have the capacity to arouse in children an awareness of the complexity and beauty of the expanding universe."

If all the good reviews and awards weren't enough, *My Side of the Mountain* is also a favorite among teachers. Sam's adventure in the Catskill Mountains is at the top of many schools' recommended-reading lists.

What is perhaps most remarkable about *My Side of the Mountain* is its long life. Published in 1959, this book was read widely when it first hit bookstores. It is impressive that today's kids are just as fascinated by Sam's adventure as readers were some forty-five years ago. Sam's timeless tale is sure to entertain budding naturalists and adventure seekers for generations to come. A reviewer from *The Horn Book* called *My Side of the Mountain* "An extraordinary book. . . . It will be read year after year."

Thinking about what others think of
My Side of the Mountain

- Do you think this book deserved a Newbery Honor?
- Do you think a twelve-year-old could really survive in the wilderness as well as Sam did?
- Why do you think this book is still so popular today?

Glossary

Here are some of the words used in *My Side of the Mountain.* Some may be new to you or used in new ways. Understanding their meanings will make it easier for you to read and appreciate the novel.

barometer an instrument that measures changes in air pressure and indicates when the weather is going to change

bellow to shout or roar

bough a tree branch

brooding worrying or thinking about one's problems

combustible capable of catching fire

dale a small valley

deadfall a mass of fallen trees; an animal trap

fell to cut, knock, or bring down

flint a piece of quartz that, when struck by steel, creates a spark

furtive done in a secretive way

gangplank a bridge used to get on and off a docked ship

gorge a deep, narrow passage through land

hemlock an evergreen tree from the pine family

jess a short strap secured to the leg of a hawk, usually along with a ring for attaching a leash

loam loose, rich soil

marksmanship skill in shooting

perch a branch where a bird sits or nests

pewee a type of bird that feeds on insects

plumage a bird's feathers

poach to hunt illegally

preen to smooth or groom oneself

primitive in an early stage of development

sagely wisely

sanguine optimistic, confident

savory tasty

scant in insufficient supply

snare a trap that entangles birds or other animals, usually with a noose

tether to tie or fasten in order to restrain

thunderhead a rounded mass of clouds that often appears before a thunderstorm

tubers fleshy underground stems or roots, like a potato

vengeance an action that is taken to pay back someone for harm that that person inflicted on you or someone you care about

venison the edible meat of a deer

ventilate to allow fresh air into a place and to allow stale air to escape

whittle to carve something out of wood by chipping off small pieces

Jean Craighead George on Writing

"I first became aware of the delights of the natural world when my father, an entomologist, presented me with what looked like a twig. When it got up and walked, my delight was such that I wrote a poem, 'To a Walking Stick.' I was in the third grade and have been writing ever since."

—Jean Craighead George

When she wants to write, Jean Craighead George begins by taking a journal into nature and taking notes about what she sees and how she feels. She wants to make sure she accurately remembers all the details so that when she writes a story, it is real and true. She even takes the time to sketch some of what she sees. George comes to know the settings so well that she is able to guide her characters in and out of believable situations in which they must use their survival instinct and skills. Her love of nature makes this easy: "Some books are harder to write than others, but the books I write from love and experience go easily. I can't wait to get up in the morning and write. At 5 A.M. I'm off to the shower, the teapot, and my

50

computer. It is quiet at that time of day, I have energy and I can write to my heart's content."

Jean Craighead George decided to become a writer when she was in the third grade. She and her brothers had spent weekends camping and observing nature with their parents. After coming home from such family outings in the wilderness, George would write about her experiences. She has said that, at first, she only wrote poems because she was "unable to sit still very long." Later, in junior high school, her writing grew into longer poems and then short stories. In college she wrote essays and, after graduating, she wrote articles as a journalist. "Finally, at the age of twenty-four," she says, "I took on the novel. I have been writing novels for young people ever since."

George is fascinated by animals, their habitats, and their interactions with people. Her experiences with nature directly influence all of the writing she does. In fact, she says that she has spent time in every location she writes about, and that all her characters are based on herself or on friends, family members, or animals she has known. "I have discovered I cannot dream up [animal] characters as incredible as the ones I meet in the wilderness," she says. George says that she's always thinking, always looking out for new ideas, always taking notes in her head. "Ideas are everywhere," she says. "Your shoes must have been many places with tales to tell. The rain coming down the windowpane is a tale to tell—and on and on."

You Be the Author!

• **The end: Or is it?:** Were you disappointed that Sam's family comes to live with him? How would you have ended the book? Rewrite it another way and see if you're satisfied with the new ending.

• **Get the scoop:** Pretend you are a reporter like Matt Spell. Write an article for the newspaper about Sam Gribley. Check out your local newspaper to see how news articles are written and try to imitate the style. How would you report on Sam's living quarters and his lifestyle? What would your headline be?

• **Change the setting:** How would Sam's story change if the setting were different? What might have happened if he had run to the desert, or to a tropical climate? What would Sam have to eat? What types of animals would he encounter? Do you think it would be easier or more difficult for Sam to survive in *your* location than it was in the Catskills? Write a few paragraphs about Sam's new survival challenges.

• **Look into the fictional future:** At the end of *My Side of the Mountain*, Sam's mother tells him that he's stuck with them until he's eighteen. What do you think Sam will do when he is really allowed to be independent? Write a short story that features Sam as he makes an important choice about his future.

- **Start a nature journal:** One way to connect with nature is to write about it. Take a few minutes each day to go outside and observe what's going on around you. Try to ignore honking horns and other modern interruptions! Take notes and make drawings of your surroundings. Write down what kinds of birds you see or make a note of which is your favorite tree or even your favorite sound. What does the wind sound like? Remember that Jean Craighead George's nature journals contain more than just words, so try drawing some of the animals you see.

- **Keep a journal of your life:** Jean Craighead George writes mostly from personal experience. She thinks that when you write about things that you care passionately about, you do your best writing. She has always kept a journal of her personal experiences so that when she sits down to write a story she will remember what the air felt like, how the trees moved, and what kind of mood it created. If you want to write, make sure to take notes of your thoughts and feelings as well as daily events. And write often so it becomes a habit!

Activities

• **Visit the library:** Just like Sam, you can go to the library and find all kinds of fascinating facts about the outdoors. If your school has a library, that's a great place to start your research. If not, ask a parent to take you to your public library. A librarian will be able to help you find exactly what you are looking for: wildlife guides, maps, books on living in nature, etc.

• **Plan a camping trip with your family:** You can get a taste of what Sam's life on the mountain was like by simply planning an outdoor adventure with friends or family. Find an area nearby that interests you. See if there are public campgrounds and, if so, find out what the rules and regulations are. Make a list of what you'll need and head on out!

If you can't get to the wilderness, make your own! With the permission of your parents, pitch a tent in the backyard or go to the roof of your building and spend the night outdoors under the stars. Bring along a nature guide or a favorite outdoor adventure story.

• **Learn to use your surroundings as your barometer:** Like Sam, pay close attention to the sky, the birds, the animals, and the water. Watch the ways that they move. Make notes when the sky shifts suddenly or when the birds' behavior changes. At the same time, observe what's happening with the weather. Is there a breeze? Does the air feel heavy? Is it raining? Based on your notes, can you see a relationship between the animals' behavior and the weather? Try to see if you can predict the weather. Can you do better than the meteorologist on the news?

• **Take a hike!:** If you can't make it to the mountains, hike around other natural settings. Take a trip to...

the botanical gardens

the zoo

a park

the city streets—just make sure to check out some trees along the way. Observe how people in the city manage to keep nature in their lives—window boxes filled with flowers, ivy growing up the sides of buildings, etc.

• **Draw the seasons:** Go outside and choose your favorite outdoor scene to draw. Then, use your knowledge of the season, plus a little imagination, to draw what that same location might look like in each season.

• **Volunteer at a nature conservatory:** If you are interested in learning how to conserve and preserve our natural surroundings, look up a local nature conservancy and see if there is a way you can get involved.

• **Visit the Catskills:** The Catskill Mountains region is a beautiful part of New York State. With more than 700,000 acres of land filled with picture-perfect waterfalls and crystal-clear streams, the Catskills are a vacation destination for thousands of people every year. Even if you and your family can't arrange to visit the area in person, you can still find out all about its vast natural resources. To do this, check out The Catskill Center for Conservation and Development at www.catskillcenter.org.

Related Reading

Other books in the Sam Gribley series:

On the Far Side of the Mountain (1990)

Frightful's Mountain (1999)

Frightful's Daughter (2002)

Other books by Jean Craighead George

Acorn Pancakes, Dandelion Salad, and 38 Other Wild Recipes (1995)

Animals Who Have Won Our Hearts (1994)

The Big Book for Our Planet (1993)

The Case of the Missing Cutthroats: An Ecological Mystery (1996)

Cliff Hanger (2002)

The Cry of the Crow: A Novel (1980)

Dear Katie, The Volcano Is a Girl (1998)

Dear Rebecca, Winter Is Here (1993)

Dipper of Copper Creek (1956)

Elephant Walk (1998)

Everglades (1995)

Everglades Wildguide (1972)

The Fire Bug Connection (1993)

The First Thanksgiving (1993)

Giraffe Trouble (1998)

Gorilla Gang (1999)

The Grizzly Bear with the Golden Ears (1982)

Hook a Fish, Catch a Mountain (1975)

How to Talk to Your Cat (1986)

How to Talk to Your Dog (1986)

Julie (1994)

Julie of the Wolves (1972)

Julie's Wolf Pack (1997)

Look to the North: A Wolf Pup Diary (1997)

The Missing 'Gator of Gumbo Limbo (1992)

Nutik & Amaroq Play Ball (2001)

Nutik, the Wolf Pup (2001)

One Day in the Desert (1983)

One Day in the Tropical Rain Forest (1990)

One Day in the Woods (1988)

Rhino Romp (1998)

Shark Beneath the Reef (1989)

Snow Bear (1999)

The Summer of the Falcon (1962)

The Talking Earth (1983)

The Tarantula in My Purse: And 172 Other Wild Pets (1997)

There's an Owl in the Shower (1995)

To Climb a Waterfall (1995)

Tree Castle Island (2002)

Vulpes the Red Fox (1948)

Water Sky (1987)

Who Really Killed Cock Robin? An Ecological Mystery (1991)

The Wounded Wolf (1978)

Survival stories—fiction

Brian's Winter by Gary Paulsen

The Cay by Theodore Taylor

Hatchet by Gary Paulsen

Island of the Blue Dolphins by Scott O'Dell

Nory Ryan's Song by Patricia Reilly Giff

The Sign of the Beaver by Elizabeth George Speare

The Swiss Family Robinson by Johann Wyss

Movies

My Side of the Mountain, Paramount Pictures, 1969.

Bibliography

Books

Cary, Alice. *Jean Craighead George* (The Learning Works Meet the Author series). Huntington Beach, California: Creative Teaching Press, Inc., 1996.

George, Jean Craighead. *My Side of the Mountain.* New York: E. P. Dutton, 1959 (reissued by Puffin Books, 1991).

Newspapers and magazines

Hopkinson, Deborah. "A nature loving author searches for paradise in the swamp," *BookPage: America's Book Review*, May 2002, p. 28.

Wilde, Susie. "Interview and review with Jean Craighead George," *BookPage: America's Book Review*, January 1995, p. 22.

Web sites

Book Sense:
   www.booksense.com

The Catskill Center for Conservation and Development:
   www.catskillcenter.org

Education Paperback Association:
   www.edupaperback.org/showauth.cfm?authid=29

Jean Craighead George:
   www.jeancraigheadgeorge.com

HarperCollins School House—*Julie of the Wolves* Teachers' Guide:
www.harperchildrens.com/schoolhouse/TeachersGuides/
jcgbio.htm

Kids Reads Author Biographies:
www.kidsreads.com/authors/au-george-jean-craighead.asp

TeenReads Author Profile:
www.teenreads.com/authors/au-george-jean.asp